Clever
Brown Mouse

Story by Jenny Giles

Illustrations by Pat DeWitt-Grush

One morning, the three little mice were playing outside.

Then they saw the cat coming.

4

"Oh, no!" cried White Mouse.

"The cat is coming to get us!"

"Run to the fence!"
said Brown Mouse.

"The cat can't get under the fence."

The mice raced over to the fence.
Then they stopped.

"We can't get under there!"
cried Gray Mouse.

"Now the cat will catch us,"
said White Mouse.

"We can get under the gate,"
said Brown Mouse. "Come on."

The mice ran under the gate.

Gray Mouse laughed.

"You were right, Brown Mouse," he said.

"We **did** get under the gate.

That was lucky!"

"And the cat can't get us now,"
smiled Brown Mouse. "We are all safe."

"No! We are not safe!"
cried White Mouse. "Look!
Here comes the dog
from next door!"

"Where can we go?"
cried Gray Mouse.

"Come with me,"
said Brown Mouse.
"Climb up the gate!"

The little mice raced up
to the top of the gate.

"Now swing on the latch like this,"
said Brown Mouse.

Down came the latch,
and the gate opened.

The cat got a big surprise!

The dog ran after the cat,

and the three little mice ran home.